ROCKFORD PUBLIC LIBRARY

Rockford, Illinois

http:\\www.rpl.rockford.org

MAR 2 2 1999

DEMCO

BIG CATS

Published by Creative Education, Inc., 123 South Broad Street, Mankato, Minnesota 56001

Printed by permission of Wildlife Education, Ltd.

ISBN 0-88682-264-5

BIG CATS

Created and Written by
John Bonnett Wexo

Zoological Consultant
Charles R. Schroeder, D.V.M.
Director Emeritus
San Diego Zoo &
San Diego Wild Animal Park

Scientific Consultant
Edward J. Maruska
Director
Cincinnati Zoological Garden

Creative Education

Art Credits

Pages Six and Seven: Davis Meltzer and Barbara Hoopes; **Pages Eight and Nine:** Barbara Hoopes; **Page Eight:** Drawing by Walter Stuart: **Pages Ten and Eleven:** Paul Breedon and Barbara Hoopes; **Pages Twelve and Thirteen:** Paul Breedon and Barbara Hoopes; **Page Thirteen: Lower Right,** Diagram by Lance Jordan and Andy Lucas; **Pages Sixteen and Seventeen:** Paul Breedon and Mark Hallett; **Page Twenty:** David Mollering, Barbara Hoopes, and Mark Hallett; **Page Twenty-one:** Drawing by Lance Jordan. **All Maps** by Andy Lucas.

Photographic Credits

Cover: John Chellman *(Animals Animals);* **Page Ten: Middle Left,** Ron Garrison/Zoological Society of San Diego; **Middle Right,** Ken Fink *(Ardea);* **Lower Left,** Dmitri Kessel *(LIFE Picture Service);* **Page Eleven: Middle Right,** John Dominis *(LIFE Picture Service);* **Page Twelve: Upper Right,** Souricat *(Animals Animals);* **Page Thirteen: Upper Right,** Ken Fink *(Ardea);* **Pages Fourteen and Fifteen:** John Daniels *(Ardea London);* **Page Sixteen: Upper Right,** Stan Wayman *(Photo Researchers);* **Lower Left,** both teeth by Charles Van Valkenburgh/Wildlife Education, Ltd.; **Page Seventeen: Lower Right,** Stan Wayman *(Photo Researchers);* **Pages Eighteen and Nineteen:** Peter Davey *(Bruce Coleman, Inc.);* **Page Twenty: Left,** C. Bevilacqua *(Istituto Geografica de Agostini);* **Page Twenty-one: Upper Left,** Bill Ray *(LIFE Picture Service);* **Upper Right,** Charles Van Valkenburgh/Wildlife Education, Ltd., Artifact Courtesy of the San Diego Museum of Man; **Lower Right,** Bettmann Archive; **Pages Twenty-two and Twenty-three:** Jen & Des Bartlett *(Bruce Coleman, Inc.).*

Our Thanks To: Barbara Shattuck *(National Geographic Magazine);* Dr. William Akersten *(George C. Page Museum of La Brea Discoveries):* Susan Hathaway *(Zoological Society of San Diego);* Dr. David Fagan; Ken Hedges *(San Diego Museum of Man);* Dallas Mayr; Barbara Ford; Lynnette Wexo.

Creative Education would like to thank Wildlife Education, Ltd., for granting them the rights to print and distribute this hardbound edition.

Contents

MOUNTAIN LION
Puma concolor

JAGUAR
Panthera onca

Big cats are among the most beautiful creatures on earth. Their strength and grace, combined with their often secretive natures, have fascinated people for ages.

All of the cats shown on these pages are popularly known as big cats, but the scientific definition of the group eliminates some of them. Briefly, scientists say that a big cat is one that can roar but cannot purr. This includes lions, tigers, leopards, and jaguars—but *excludes* mountain lions, snow leopards,

AFRICAN LIONS
Panthera leo

LEOPARD, SPOTTED AND DARK PHASES
Panthera pardus

clouded leopards, and cheetah.

Big cats are sometimes very big. The Siberian tiger can weigh up to 770 pounds (349 kilograms), and may be 11½ feet (3½ meters) long. But some big cats can be smaller than cats that are called "little" cats.

As a group, big cats have a large range. They are found north of the Arctic Circle, and in steaming tropical jungles. Every continent but Europe, Australia, and Antarctica has its big cats.

SNOW LEOPARD
Uncia uncia

CLOUDED LEOPARD
Neofelis nebulosa

CHEETAH
Acinonyx jubatus

SIBERIAN TIGER
Panthera tigris

Big cats are beautifully constructed

for the role they play in nature. There must be hunters to keep animal populations in balance, and for this purpose big cats are well equipped. Their bodies are heavily muscled, well armed, and powerful.

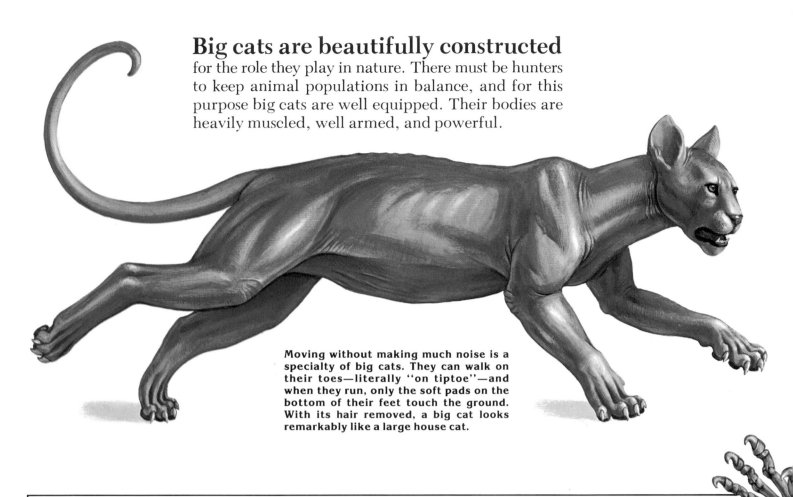

Moving without making much noise is a specialty of big cats. They can walk on their toes—literally "on tiptoe"—and when they run, only the soft pads on the bottom of their feet touch the ground. With its hair removed, a big cat looks remarkably like a large house cat.

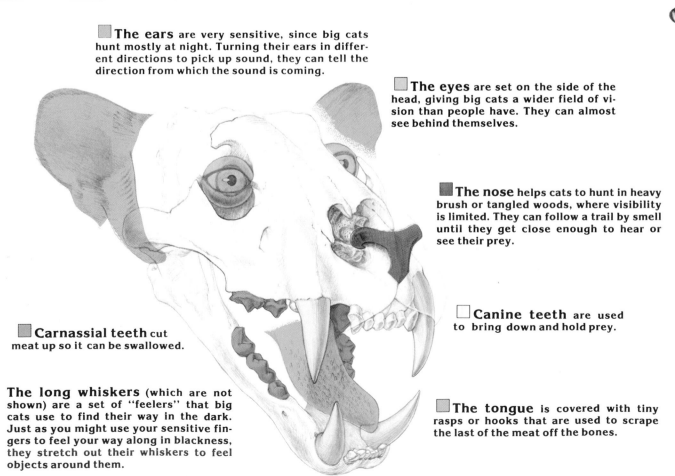

The ears are very sensitive, since big cats hunt mostly at night. Turning their ears in different directions to pick up sound, they can tell the direction from which the sound is coming.

The eyes are set on the side of the head, giving big cats a wider field of vision than people have. They can almost see behind themselves.

The nose helps cats to hunt in heavy brush or tangled woods, where visibility is limited. They can follow a trail by smell until they get close enough to hear or see their prey.

Carnassial teeth cut meat up so it can be swallowed.

Canine teeth are used to bring down and hold prey.

The long whiskers (which are not shown) are a set of "feelers" that big cats use to find their way in the dark. Just as you might use your sensitive fingers to feel your way along in blackness, they stretch out their whiskers to feel objects around them.

The tongue is covered with tiny rasps or hooks that are used to scrape the last of the meat off the bones.

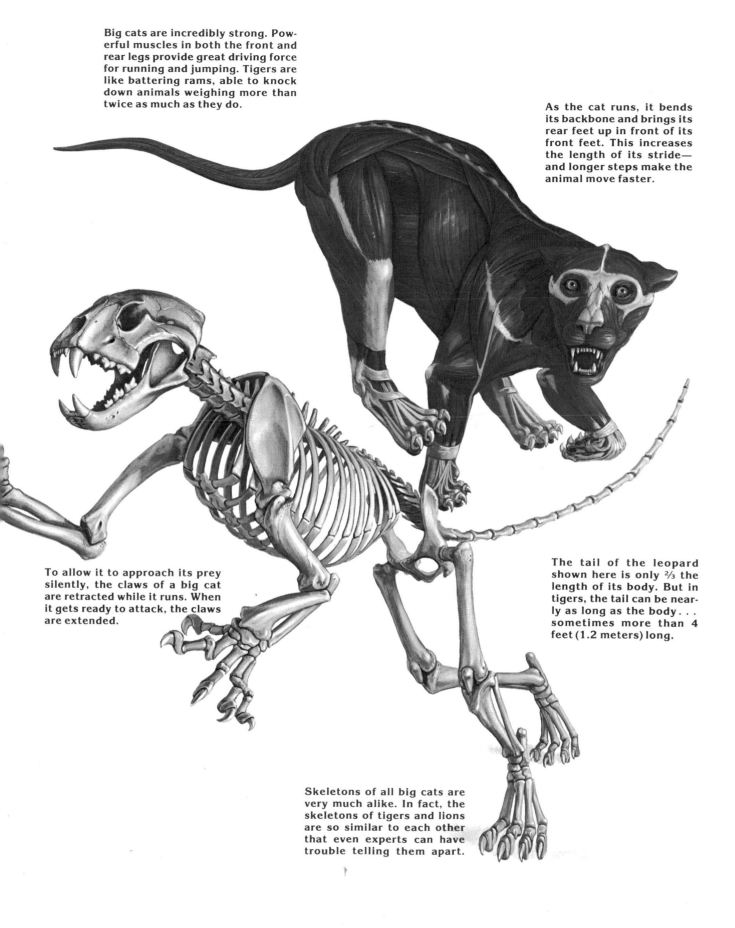

Big cats are incredibly strong. Powerful muscles in both the front and rear legs provide great driving force for running and jumping. Tigers are like battering rams, able to knock down animals weighing more than twice as much as they do.

As the cat runs, it bends its backbone and brings its rear feet up in front of its front feet. This increases the length of its stride—and longer steps make the animal move faster.

To allow it to approach its prey silently, the claws of a big cat are retracted while it runs. When it gets ready to attack, the claws are extended.

The tail of the leopard shown here is only ⅔ the length of its body. But in tigers, the tail can be nearly as long as the body... sometimes more than 4 feet (1.2 meters) long.

Skeletons of all big cats are very much alike. In fact, the skeletons of tigers and lions are so similar to each other that even experts can have trouble telling them apart.

9

Leopards and jaguars are the two spotted members of the big cat family, and this is not the only similarity between them. Both are equally at home in a wide variety of settings—swamps, forests, mountains, grasslands, and even desert areas. Both can survive on a wide variety of different food items, from large herd animals down to insects. And both have maintained large ranges despite the destructive activities of people.

The key to the success of both the jaguar and the leopard has been the ability of both animals to adapt to changing conditions.

Leopards are the smallest of the big cats, with an average weight of only 100 pounds (46 kilograms). They are also the most secretive and adaptable members of the group...and they have been most successful at staying out of man's way. As a result, they may have a better chance of surviving than the others.

Dark leopards and jaguars are found most often in deep forests and jungles, and it seems likely that their color helps them to hide in shadows. In open country, animals of lighter color are more often found.

Both jaguars and leopards may be born with dark, nearly black coats. If you look closely, you will still see spots in the coat, but the dark background tends to hide them.

The range of jaguars is not as large as it once was. But they can still be found in remote areas from northern Mexico to almost the tip of South America.

Jaguars like water as much as tigers do —and perhaps even more. They will chase prey into the water, and sometimes swim around looking for turtles, fish, and crocodiles to catch.

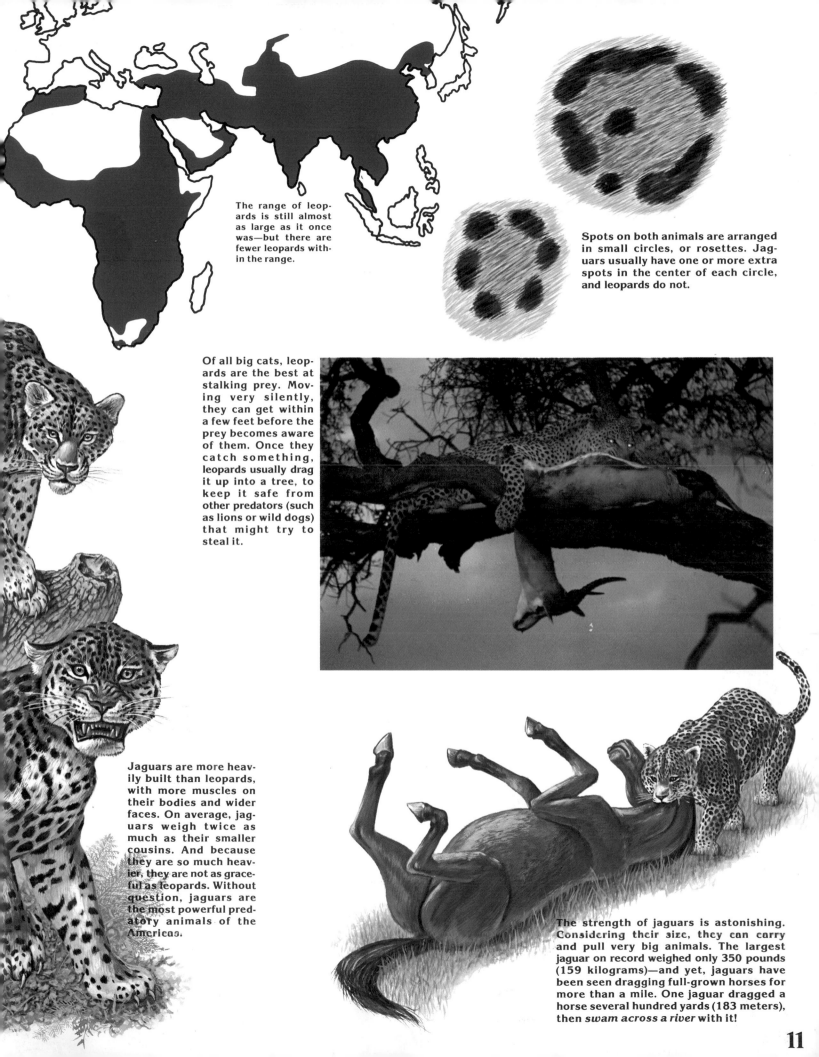

The range of leopards is still almost as large as it once was—but there are fewer leopards within the range.

Spots on both animals are arranged in small circles, or rosettes. Jaguars usually have one or more extra spots in the center of each circle, and leopards do not.

Of all big cats, leopards are the best at stalking prey. Moving very silently, they can get within a few feet before the prey becomes aware of them. Once they catch something, leopards usually drag it up into a tree, to keep it safe from other predators (such as lions or wild dogs) that might try to steal it.

Jaguars are more heavily built than leopards, with more muscles on their bodies and wider faces. On average, jaguars weigh twice as much as their smaller cousins. And because they are so much heavier, they are not as graceful as leopards. Without question, jaguars are the most powerful predatory animals of the Americas.

The strength of jaguars is astonishing. Considering their size, they can carry and pull very big animals. The largest jaguar on record weighed only 350 pounds (159 kilograms)—and yet, jaguars have been seen dragging full-grown horses for more than a mile. One jaguar dragged a horse several hundred yards (183 meters), then *swam across a river* with it!

Lions are different from the other big cats in several important ways. All of the others are solitary— they live alone most of the time and usually hunt alone as well. But lions live in groups called "prides" that can include as many as 35 lions. Unlike other big cats, adult lions do not have stripes or spots on their coats. And while tigers, leopards, and jaguars will often live in forests and swamps, African lions prefer the wide-open spaces.

It could be that life on the open plains has forced the lion to adopt a different method of living and hunting.

When lions have just had a meal, they become very lazy. They pay no attention to nearby animals that they would normally chase. The animals know this and don't run away—but they keep their eyes on the lions, all the same.

A lion's roar can carry for more than 5 miles (8 kilometers).

Only male lions have manes, which can vary in color from very dark to very light brown.

Lions spend most of the day sleeping or lying in the shade relaxing. It has been said that the lion is "the laziest animal in Africa."

Lion cubs are born in litters of four or less, as a rule. When young, their coats are spotted. But as they grow older, the spots disappear.

In the past, lions had a much larger range. Less than 2,000 years ago, there were lions in southeastern Europe. Today, they are limited to parts of Africa and a very small game preserve at Gir in India.

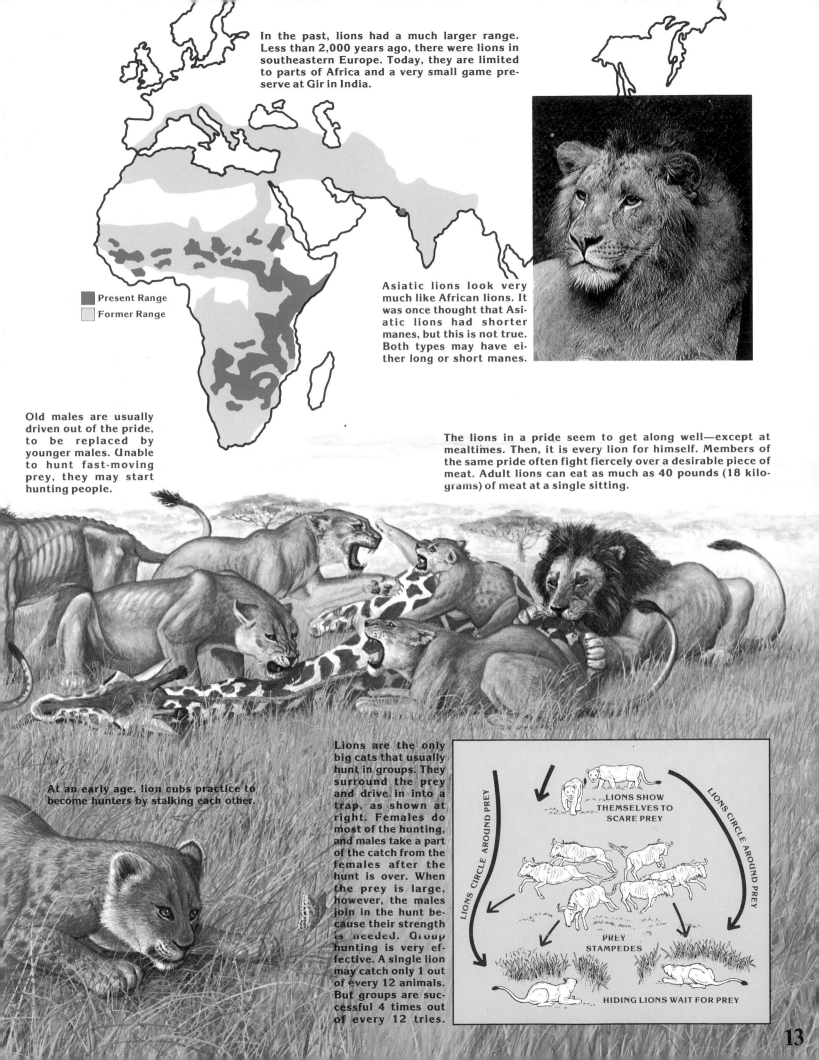

Present Range
Former Range

Asiatic lions look very much like African lions. It was once thought that Asiatic lions had shorter manes, but this is not true. Both types may have either long or short manes.

Old males are usually driven out of the pride, to be replaced by younger males. Unable to hunt fast-moving prey, they may start hunting people.

The lions in a pride seem to get along well—except at mealtimes. Then, it is every lion for himself. Members of the same pride often fight fiercely over a desirable piece of meat. Adult lions can eat as much as 40 pounds (18 kilograms) of meat at a single sitting.

At an early age, lion cubs practice to become hunters by stalking each other.

Lions are the only big cats that usually hunt in groups. They surround the prey and drive in into a trap, as shown at right. Females do most of the hunting, and males take a part of the catch from the females after the hunt is over. When the prey is large, however, the males join in the hunt because their strength is needed. Group hunting is very effective. A single lion may catch only 1 out of every 12 animals. But groups are successful 4 times out of every 12 tries.

LIONS CIRCLE AROUND PREY

LIONS CIRCLE AROUND PREY

LIONS SHOW THEMSELVES TO SCARE PREY

PREY STAMPEDES

HIDING LIONS WAIT FOR PREY

These lion cubs look ready to cuddle and spend most of their time playing.

Tigers are often called the most beautiful of the big cats, as well as the most powerful and most dangerous to man. Their reputation for beauty and power is well deserved. There can be few things as elegant as a tiger's striped coat, and they are the most muscular of the big cats. But the threat they pose to man has been greatly exaggerated.

No two tigers have the same pattern of stripes. Face markings are so distinctive that they can be used to tell one tiger from another.

If tigers had no stripes, they might starve to death. Since they are not fast runners, they must get close to their prey to have even a hope of catching it. Their stripes hide them from sight well enough for them to get close. Even so, tigers catch only one out of every 20 animals they go after.

Tigers have the largest canine teeth of any meat-eating land animal. But even the tooth of a very large tiger looks small next to the 8-inch (20-centimeter) tooth of a gigantic extinct Sabretooth cat.

When the weather gets warm, tigers can often be found in the water cooling themselves off. Unlike most cats, tigers love the water and swim well. They can easily swim 3 or 4 miles (4½ or 6½ kilometers).

16

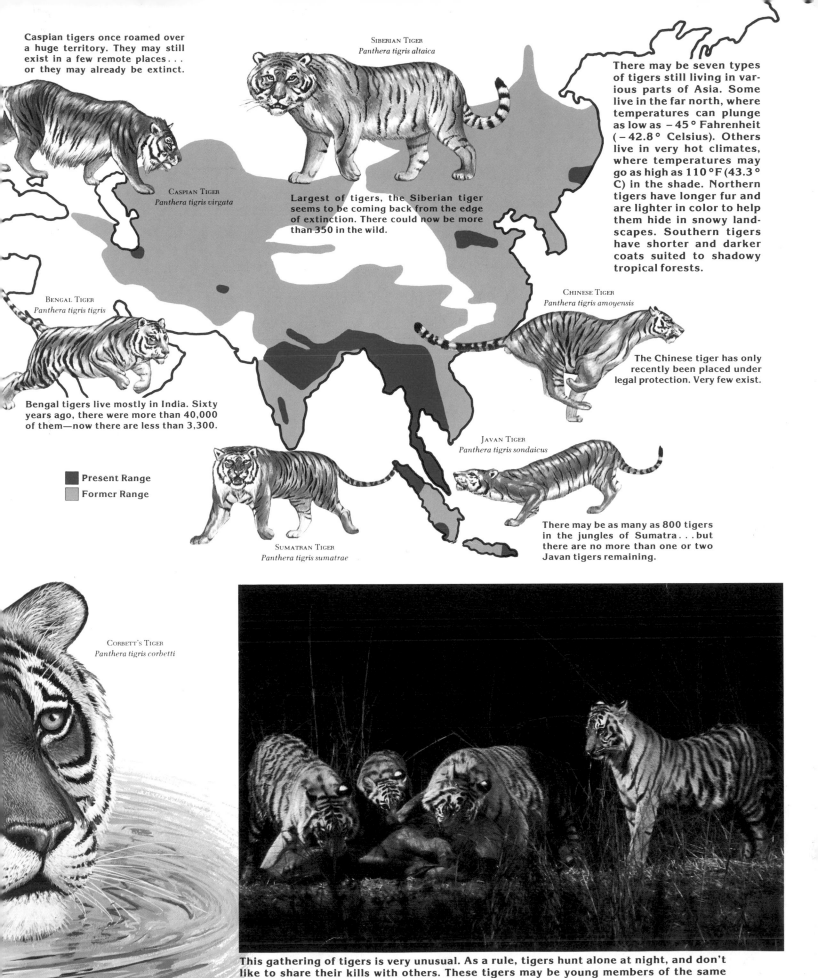

Caspian tigers once roamed over a huge territory. They may still exist in a few remote places... or they may already be extinct.

SIBERIAN TIGER
Panthera tigris altaica

CASPIAN TIGER
Panthera tigris virgata

Largest of tigers, the Siberian tiger seems to be coming back from the edge of extinction. There could now be more than 350 in the wild.

There may be seven types of tigers still living in various parts of Asia. Some live in the far north, where temperatures can plunge as low as −45° Fahrenheit (−42.8° Celsius). Others live in very hot climates, where temperatures may go as high as 110°F (43.3° C) in the shade. Northern tigers have longer fur and are lighter in color to help them hide in snowy landscapes. Southern tigers have shorter and darker coats suited to shadowy tropical forests.

BENGAL TIGER
Panthera tigris tigris

Bengal tigers live mostly in India. Sixty years ago, there were more than 40,000 of them—now there are less than 3,300.

CHINESE TIGER
Panthera tigris amoyensis

The Chinese tiger has only recently been placed under legal protection. Very few exist.

■ Present Range
▨ Former Range

JAVAN TIGER
Panthera tigris sondaicus

SUMATRAN TIGER
Panthera tigris sumatrae

There may be as many as 800 tigers in the jungles of Sumatra... but there are no more than one or two Javan tigers remaining.

CORBETT'S TIGER
Panthera tigris corbetti

This gathering of tigers is very unusual. As a rule, tigers hunt alone at night, and don't like to share their kills with others. These tigers may be young members of the same family that have not yet gone out on their own. When fully grown, a tiger needs about 15 pounds (6.8 kilograms) of food every day to survive.

CHEETAH

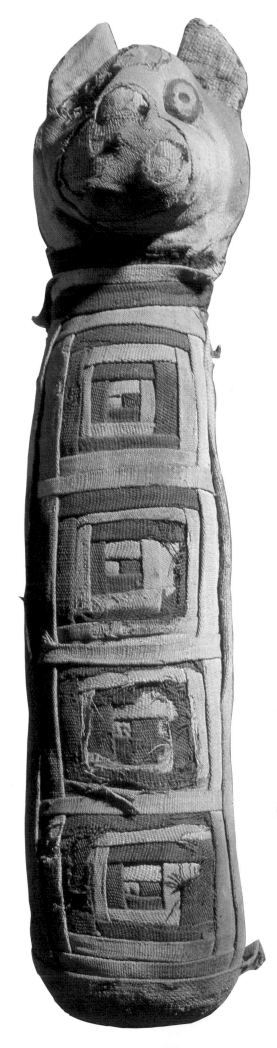

People have loved and feared big cats throughout history. Ancient tribes worshiped them. The Egyptians, who were probably the first to domesticate small cats, mummified them (as shown at left), and kept big cats in zoos as symbols of royal power. Nations have placed pictures of them on flags, and kings and emperors have worn their skins as part of their royal regalia. To this day, in the minds of most people, big cats stand for courage and majesty.

The cheetah is no longer classified as a big cat, but for centuries it was known as "the hunting leopard," and was used by man to help bring down game. Running at speeds exceeding 60 miles per hour (96½ kilometers per hour), this fastest of all land animals would catch the prey and hold it until the human hunters arrived. The emperor Kublai Khan was said to have owned 1,000 hunting cheetah.

Even though big cats are in danger throughout the world, and most of them have been protected by law, illegal hunting goes on. Certain selfish people care more about showing off with a spotted coat than they do about the fate of these beautiful animals. At left, a game warden with a pile of illegal skins.

To the ancient peoples of South America, the strength and beauty of the jaguar qualified it as one of the highest gods. This handsome pot from the Moche culture of coastal Peru shows a jaguar holding a dog.

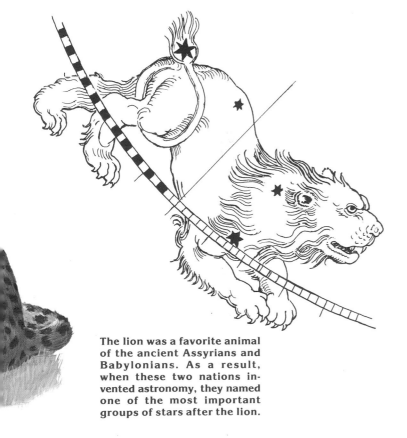

The lion was a favorite animal of the ancient Assyrians and Babylonians. As a result, when these two nations invented astronomy, they named one of the most important groups of stars after the lion.

Until recently, great prestige has been the reward for killing a tiger—and the bigger the tiger, the greater the prestige. To please high-ranking hunters, a special tape measure, with only 11 inches (28 centimeters) to the foot (30.5 centimeters), was used to measure their tigers. Many a 10-foot (3-meter) tiger became an 11-foot (3⅓-meter) tiger in this way.

21

The future of big cats is up to us. If
people do not take action to save them, they
will surely be extinct in the wild within 20 years.

It is people, after all, who created the prob-
lem. As the human population has continued
to grow, more and more food has been needed. To produce the food, more and more land
is taken from the wild and turned into farm
land. As more and more land is taken, there is
room for fewer and fewer wild animals. And
big cats find it harder and harder to find any-
thing to eat.

Tigers are the most endangered of all. Fifty
years ago, there were more than 100,000 tigers in Asia. Today, there are fewer than 6,500.
The Bali Tiger has become extinct. The Caspian tiger may also be gone. The Javan tiger
is sure to disappear within a few years. And
the fate of the Chinese tiger is uncertain.

Lions are also in serious trouble. One hundred years ago, they could be found throughout Africa and over much of Asia. Today,
they are gone from South Africa and North
Africa, and they will soon be gone from West
Africa as well. Of the once huge Asian population, fewer than 200 remain in a small preserve in India.

Incredible as it may seem, hunting of big
cats still goes on. They are protected by law in
most countries, but the value of spotted and
striped skins is so high that illegal hunting is
inevitable. For a poor farmer, the price that a
trader will pay for a single tiger skin is enough
to feed his family for years. And so he kills the
beautiful beast.

What can we do to stop all this? To put an
end to hunting, we can support our govern-
ment and wildlife groups in their efforts to
have the sale of big cat skins stopped around
the world. If the market for skins in rich
countries is closed, there will be no incentive
for people in poor countries to kill the animals.

To save big cats from destruction of their
living space, we can help organizations like
the World Wildlife Fund to establish preserves
where big cats and other animals will be safe
from man. We can lend our voices — and our
financial support — to the growing clamor to
save the big cats.

Index